THE LITTLE BOOK OF
MEDITATIONS

THE LITTLE BOOK OF MEDITATIONS

Andrews McMeel Publishing
a division of Andrews McMeel Universal
1130 Walnut Street, Kansas City, Missouri 64106

www.andrewsmcmeel.com

First published in 2019 by Summersdale Publishers Ltd.
46 West Street,
Chichester, West Sussex
PO19 1RP, UK.

19 20 21 22 23 RLP 10 9 8 7 6 5 4 3 2 1

ISBN: 978-1-5248-5200-9

Library of Congress Control Number: 2019936826

Text: Gilly Pickup
Editor: Kevin Kotur
Production Manager: Tamara Haus
Production Editor: Julie Railsback

ATTENTION: SCHOOLS AND BUSINESSES
Andrews McMeel books are available at quantity discounts with bulk purchase for educational, business, or sales promotional use. For information, please e-mail the Andrews McMeel Publishing Special Sales Department: specialsales@amuniversal.com

THE LITTLE BOOK OF
MEDITATIONS

Gilly Pickup

Andrews McMeel
PUBLISHING®

CONTENTS

MEDITATION EXPLAINED
A Brief Introduction

WHAT IS MEDITATION?

In simple terms, meditation is a process of awareness leading to a state of consciousness that brings serenity and clarity of mind. Meditation enables the practitioner (i.e., you) to reach a different state of consciousness from the normal waking state. This means that when you master the art of meditation, whatever you do, you do it more effectively.

Maybe you know someone who says, "I've tried meditating, but it's no use—I just can't seem to get the hang of it." If you ask them why, they may say, "My mind won't stop buzzing. I have so many things to think about. I can't clear my head and get rid of random thoughts, so meditation isn't going to work for me." Of course, it is true that sometimes when beginners struggle to control or reduce their flow of thoughts, they become disillusioned and think meditation won't work for them. But it's perfectly OK to still have thoughts, because through practice you learn to observe them without judgment. Meditation is a skill that you can develop, just like playing the violin, baking a cake, learning to speak French, or anything else.

Meditation does not mean you have to "turn off" thoughts in your mind; it is about establishing a healthier relationship with your mind. After all, your mind does not come with an "off" switch—it will never stop producing thoughts.

Meditation is about balance, wakefulness, and awareness; it is not about forcing something to be done in a certain way. The restless, unconscious, repetitive mind is simply a habit, and we all know that habits can be changed or broken. Sooner or later your ability to meditate will become natural to you, and it will be one of the most enjoyable and refreshing parts of your day.

We have all experienced the endless chatter that goes on in our minds: the continual *What ifs, Whys, Will I?, Should I?, I can't forget*—it is a never-ending list. The trouble is, this constant "silent noise" in our head prevents us from embracing peace and mental quiet. Meditation is an excellent way to calm the relentless noise and enable us to bring mental clarity into our lives, thereby succumbing to some peace and quiet, which is so important to our physical and mental health.

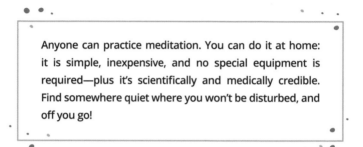

Anyone can practice meditation. You can do it at home: it is simple, inexpensive, and no special equipment is required—plus it's scientifically and medically credible. Find somewhere quiet where you won't be disturbed, and off you go!

The goal of meditation is to achieve inner peace; during meditation your body will also become rested and relaxed. When you cultivate a peaceful mind, you feel good and positive within. Meditation brings mental, emotional, and spiritual balance, which is the key to enlightenment.

Meditation is essentially relaxation time, so it should be practiced when you know you won't be disturbed. The hours of sunrise and sunset, when nature transitions between day and night, are ideal times to meditate.

WAYS TO MEDITATE

There is no single way to meditate—there are lots. Among the most popular is focused-attention, or mindful meditation, where you concentrate on something specific. This could be your breathing or a certain sensation in your body, for example. The point of this type of meditation is to focus on one thing; when your attention wanders, keep bringing it back to that focal point.

TAKE YOUR TIME

Many people may find meditation challenging at first, but as is the case with anything we start to learn, it takes time. Sometimes this has to do with the feeling of expectation. When we try to meditate and feel that nothing is happening, it is easy to lose enthusiasm. We forget that it is not about *making* something happen but simply about *being* present for the exercise. Some people get caught up in thinking too much about the experience or overanalyzing it. They may have an idea in their mind of what meditation is supposed to be, how it is supposed to feel, and that if their experience doesn't match the ideal, they are doing something wrong.

It is a fallacy that your mind is supposed to be empty of all thoughts while meditating. This is not the case. It is normal to experience a gaggle of thoughts when you first start—and of course, the more you try to make your thoughts vanish, the more the opposite will happen.

Generally speaking, many people find the easiest way to begin meditating is to focus on their breathing.

BECOME FAMILIAR

Loosely translated, the Tibetan term for meditation, *gom*, means "to become familiar with." So in other words, meditation is a means of becoming more familiar with what is going on in your mind and with the types of thoughts that pop into your head throughout your day.

Commitment to a regular, daily practice is more important than method or technique.

YOUR DAILY DOSE

Make up your mind to meditate daily. "Ah," you say, "I am always so busy—I'm not sure I can squeeze anything else into my packed schedule every day." Well, if it makes it easier, think of meditation as an investment: an investment in you, your health, and your well-being. Allow nothing but the most demanding situation to distract you from your practice. Meditation is a worthy investment that, in time, will bring enormous benefits to many areas of your life.

And you know, it doesn't need to take up too much of your time; even if you can only manage sessions of five minutes, that's enough to start with. Later, you may find a longer meditation session—around twenty minutes—helps you relax more (although there are those for whom brief five- to ten-minute sessions are enough). Experiment with different session lengths until you find your comfort zone.

FIND TIME

When you think about it, it is strange that we never have a problem finding time for things we enjoy doing. This means that when you establish a positive experience with daily meditation, even if it is for only a few minutes, it won't be long before you find you want to meditate for more extended sessions—and it won't feel like a bore or a chore. Indeed, it will be something you look forward to.

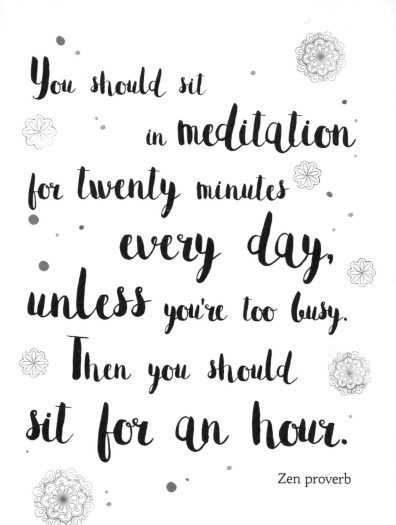

You should sit in meditation for twenty minutes every day, unless you're too busy. Then you should sit for an hour.

Zen proverb

HOW TO MEDITATE
A Guide for Beginners

WHEN TO MEDITATE

If at all possible, try to meditate at the same time every day, as this establishes a routine. Some people prefer to practice in the early morning, because when you have just awoken from sleep you have not yet become consumed with the day's stresses. That is also the time when your mind is refreshed and you *should* feel most energetic. However, as is the case with most things in life, that doesn't work for everyone—some people prefer to meditate in their coffee break or lunch hour if they have a quiet space they can go to, or after work has finished for the day. Remember, it's your call, so just go with whatever time of day or evening works best for you. If you try to force yourself to meditate at a time that doesn't feel comfortable for you, it will feel like an extra inconvenience in your day-to-day routine.

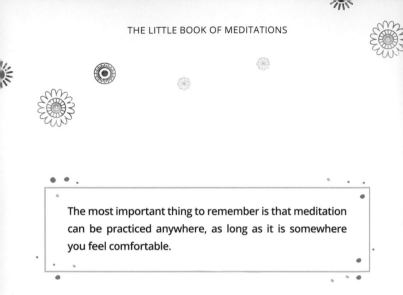

> The most important thing to remember is that meditation can be practiced anywhere, as long as it is somewhere you feel comfortable.

There are plenty of ways to get started with meditation. As a beginner, if you feel that you might benefit from guidance, try an online video, download an app, or find a face-to-face guided meditation session.

THERE ARE TWO
MISTAKES ONE CAN
MAKE ALONG THE
ROAD TO TRUTH: NOT
GOING ALL THE WAY,
AND NOT STARTING.

Buddhist proverb

You don't need to have a guru, and it's not essential to spend lots of time in an ashram or retreat to learn the art. You don't need to be particularly spiritual, clever, or medically minded. Anyone can meditate.

BEGIN WITH A CLEAR HEAD

Like everything else, the more you practice meditation, the more benefits you will experience. One thing to remember, though, is that you should be in a neutral state of mind before you begin. If there is something that you need to take care of first, take some time to do that before you start—otherwise it will cause mental nagging.

WHAT TO WEAR

When you are ready to start your session, wear comfortable clothes. One main goal of meditation is to calm the mind; this can be difficult if you feel uncomfortable, so avoid wearing restrictive clothing such as jeans or anything tight. Loose, exercise-type attire is ideal, and make sure you remove your shoes. Wear a sweater or use a blanket if you are meditating in a cool environment; you don't want the sense of feeling cold to consume your thoughts.

Don't wait until you have twenty minutes or longer to meditate: even five minutes can make a difference. Of course, it is nice to meditate for longer stretches, but as with any exercise program, the effects are cumulative.

Meditation isn't about emptying the mind, but instead noticing your thoughts and shifting your attention to your breathing.

FIRST STEP

First of all, find somewhere quiet. It doesn't have to be a totally silent place, just an area or a room where you won't be distracted or disturbed during the time you put aside to meditate. Try to find a special place for your meditation sessions, away from daily distractions: if, for instance, you sit on the chair you usually use when you watch TV, or the chair that you use at your office desk, you might feel like starting on other activities instead. Having a separate space, however small, means your mind and body will associate it with your meditation practice.

Decide how long you want to meditate for. Although a fifteen-minute session is generally recommended, when you start out you can practice for as little as four to five minutes at a time. It's up to you. If you want to, you can build up slowly to fifteen or twenty minutes. Turn off the TV and switch off your phone. If you like to listen to music, opt for something calm—even repetitive—to avoid disturbing your concentration.

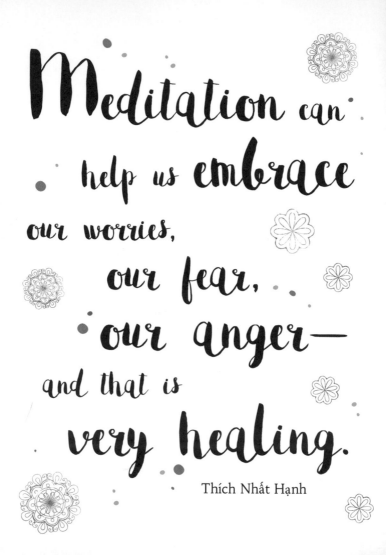

Meditation can help us embrace our worries, our fear, our anger— and that is very healing.

Thích Nhất Hạnh

SOOTHE YOUR SENSES

If you like candles, you could add them to your space—they enhance the atmosphere and create a feeling of relaxation. It's probably best to stick to LED candles for the sake of fire safety, and you can now buy scented versions of these: aromas can have a positive effect on how you feel. A houseplant or flowers can also cultivate a feeling of restfulness and increase the sensation of peace and beauty in your life.

If you meditate in the evening and your room is artificially lit, perhaps you could use a dimmer switch to adjust the lighting levels. It all helps to enhance that feeling of relaxation.

RIGHT ON TIME

Set a timer. As well as making sure you meditate for long enough, using a timer means you won't have to interrupt your practice to check how long you have left. As you build confidence in your meditation, extend the timer every session by thirty seconds until you are meditating for five or ten minutes at a time. No timer? Look for websites or apps that will time your sessions. Choose something with a quiet alarm—you don't want to be startled by an unexpected sound.

You don't need to be religious to meditate. Meditation and religion are different things, so it is possible to have one without the other. Meditation can be practiced without any religious involvement.

SECOND STEP

Sit or lie down comfortably. Allow your muscles to relax, except those that are supporting your head, neck and back. Keep your mouth closed, but relax your jaw—don't clench it. Keep your tongue lightly touching the roof of your mouth.

If you don't have a meditation chair or meditation cushion (sometimes called a *zafu*), any comfortable pillow or cushion is absolutely fine. Sitting upright without back support helps you to concentrate on your breathing as you inhale and exhale. If you choose to sit in a conventional chair, try not to lean back in it. Stay as upright as possible, if you are able to do so, and place both feet on the floor. This helps to keep you alert. Don't strain: position your legs in a way that is comfortable for you. Extend them in front of you or cross them beneath you if you're using a cushion on the ground. Contrary to what some say, you don't have to sit in the lotus position (*padmasana*) to meditate.

THE LOTUS POSITION

For those unfamilar with the lotus position (*padmasana*), this means sitting with your legs crossed and placing each leg on top of the opposite thigh. It does create a stable foundation for your body, and there is something reassuring about sitting in the same way as the great meditators of old. Of course, it may be difficult for some people to do this, and even with practice you may never manage it. Don't force it if it doesn't come naturally. You could, if you wish, try the half-lotus position, as it's a bit easier to manage than the full lotus. It involves placing one foot on the opposite thigh and the other foot on the floor underneath the opposite thigh. Make sure that both knees touch the floor. Easier still is the quarter lotus, where one of your feet rests on the calf of your other leg.

SEEK STILLNESS

Some practitioners who choose to meditate in the evening like to sit on a chair and meditate while soaking their feet in a bowl of warm, soapy water. This can help soak away the stresses of the day. Regardless of how you prefer to sit, though, try to keep as still as you possibly can. Since the mind and body are interconnected, moving the body tends to keep the mind moving as well. Stay still, and you are halfway to a quiet mind.

You may find it helpful to rest your hands in your lap, palms facing upward, with your right hand on top of your left. However, if that doesn't feel comfortable for you, you can rest your hands on your knees or leave them hanging down by your sides.

It's easy to feel confused when trying to find the perfect space and choose the perfect position, but all of this is really incidental. Meditation should feel natural and easy, even if that means just sitting on a park bench during your lunch break with birdsong as an accompaniment.

Meditation is about developing calmness, practicing mindfulness, and decluttering your mind of negative thoughts.

THIRD STEP

Some teachers and books say you should keep your eyes open while meditating. Others say they should be closed. In reality, it doesn't matter one iota if your eyes are wide open or tight shut. If you are a beginner, it is probably easier to meditate with your eyes closed, which makes it easier to block out any visual distractions. The downside of having your eyes closed is that it can be conducive to falling asleep. You could alternate between closing and opening your eyes, closing them to concentrate and opening them to remain present and awake. Whatever you choose, it is important to be aware of your surroundings: pay attention to what you hear, feel any sensations that may be flowing through your body, and let any thoughts flit through your mind.

FOURTH STEP

Just breathe naturally with your mouth closed, while inhaling and exhaling through your nose. Focus your attention on your breathing and observe the rising and falling sensation it creates in your body. Why does focusing on our breathing help? Because it means you become aware of the mind's tendency to jump from one thing to another. The simple discipline of concentration brings us back to the present and all the richness of experience that it contains. If your mind wanders—and no doubt it will, particularly as you start out on your meditation journey—just bring your attention back to your breathing and continue. At this stage it is almost impossible to stop random thoughts or ideas from pushing their way into your mind, so don't worry about it.

Be alert yet relaxed when you meditate. Yes, it may be a contradiction in terms, but it is necessary to stay alert to be in the moment. Plus, if you allow yourself to become too relaxed, you may doze off!

Concentrate on your breathing in the way that's most comfortable for you. Some people like to focus on how their lungs expand and contract, while others may think about how air passes through their nose. You might even focus on the sound of your breathing. Just bring yourself to a state of mind where you are focused on some aspect of your breath. By concentrating on your inhalations and exhalations, you will find that other thoughts from the outside world fall away without you having to worry about how to ignore them.

BREATHING

For a few moments, pay close attention to the quality of each breath. Is it deep? Is it shallow? Maybe it is slow or fast, long or short. Start to count your breaths silently— one as you inhale, two as you exhale, three on the next inhalation, and so on, up to ten. Then start again at one. While doing this, thoughts may come into your mind. That's OK. When you realize your mind has wandered, just gently guide your attention back to your breathing. If you remember which number you had counted up to, you could start again from there or go back to one and begin again. If you can manage to do it, try to exhale for longer than you inhale. By getting rid of more used air, you are making much more space for fresh air to fill your lungs.

ATTENTION

Even when you become an experienced practitioner of meditation, you may still find that your thoughts will wander. Perhaps you will start thinking about what you have to do later, about something that is taking place at work, what you intend to cook for dinner, that you have some clothes to collect from the dry cleaner's, that you promised to catch up with a friend. Don't worry, just nudge your focus back to your breathing and allow intrusive thoughts to go away. In fact, a useful goal for beginners is being able to redirect your attention back to your point of focus without criticizing yourself.

As soon as you start
paying attention to your
breath, you are more in
touch with your inner world,
more in touch with
the moment.

FIFTH STEP

Observe your posture and notice the sensations where your body touches the chair and your feet meet the ground. Feel your hands resting on your legs or, if you are lying down, alongside your body. Acknowledge your senses and take notice of what you can smell, hear, and taste.

Occasionally you might feel cramps, pain, or tingling in your arms or legs. If you do, make sure your posture is correct. Maybe you haven't realized that you are slouching or that you're tensing your muscles. If you have been sitting in one position for too long, you can get pins and needles. Although this sensation usually clears up fairly quickly, you can prevent it by doing stretching exercises.

However, if you are meditating in a comfortable, correct position and you still feel aches, cramps, or muscular tension, know that this is not an uncommon sensation for some people to experience—this is a sign that past traumas stored within the body are gradually being released. It does not mean you are not meditating correctly—it means that your practice is effective and correct, and you are healing the old conditioning.

Just carry on with your practice and try not to pay too much heed to the physical-release process. It will come to an end when the stored stresses have been cleared away. A massage or having a bath after meditating will help to relax your body until the discomfort clears.

Some people find that practicing yoga poses before their meditation session helps make sitting much more comfortable. The cobra pose and locust pose are both good for strengthening the spine.

IT IS BETTER TO
MEDITATE A LITTLE BIT
WITH DEPTH THAN TO
MEDITATE LONG WITH
THE MIND RUNNING
HERE AND THERE.

Paramahansa
Yogananda

SIXTH STEP

Slowly turn your mind inward. Scan your body from the bottom of your feet to the top of your head. "Scanning" the body means starting your meditation practice by bringing your awareness to your feet and toes before mentally travelling up to your ankles, calves, knees, thighs, and stomach. Continue to mentally move upwards to finally reach the head. Observe any sites of tension. Don't try to change what you find; simply take notice of it. Now observe which parts of your body feel relaxed. Notice any thoughts that arise, but don't try to change them. There is no need to worry about your mind not being clear. Many people think meditation is all about clearing your mind, emptying it of all thoughts. It isn't. Just practice focusing your attention, and practice again when your mind wanders. Continue until the timer sounds.

Even with just a few minutes of practice daily, meditating has profound effects. Stay with it; don't give up; give it time. As with most things, the more you put in, the more you get back.

SEVENTH STEP

Now that your meditation session is over, don't rush to open your eyes. Open them slowly and gradually and take time to become aware of yourself and your surroundings. Sit quietly for a few minutes and stretch your arms and legs gently before returning to your usual activities. Be gentle with yourself. Don't rush to start something, whatever that may be. Consider what you are going to do next—whether making a cup of coffee, taking the dog for a walk, or catching the bus to work. Hold on to that feeling of calm you created during your meditation—keep it close and take it with you to your next task. Remind yourself throughout the day of the feeling that focused attention during meditation gave you. Take some deep breaths and recall the experience. Notice how that makes you feel.

> Ideally, meditation can be done first thing in the morning and then again at the end of the day. As you become more used to meditating, you will experience a refreshing state of natural clarity and concentration.

Meditation isn't about trying to control or quiet the mind. It is about being at ease with your mind. Don't try to force it.

LET GO OF JUDGMENT

Always keep this in mind: there is no right or wrong when you meditate. You may want to judge yourself when you become distracted or fidget—or find that your mind is wandering. These things are not bad or wrong. These are not negative experiences; they are natural. Meditation is about experiencing them and allowing them to happen.

A good time to meditate is before you sit down to a meal, though try not to do it when you are extremely hungry. If you have eaten and feel full, there is the possibility you might doze off while meditating. If you are digesting a meal, you might feel a little uncomfortable and find it difficult to concentrate.

TOGETHER OR ALONE?

If you don't feel motivated to practice meditation alone, join a meditation class. Besides finding friends with a shared interest, you'll be more driven to participate with the support of others. However you choose to meditate, though, whether together or alone, the best way to develop good meditation habits is simply to practice daily—just do it!

When meditating, don't spend your time worrying about whether or not you are doing it correctly. It could take some time for you to become skilled, and that is perfectly OK. Just keep practicing and enjoy the journey.

MEDITATION and ITS RELEVANCE TODAY

MEDITATION IN THE MODERN WORLD

Some of you reading this book may think, "How can an ancient practice such as meditation have relevance in our world today?" Well, it probably has even more relevance than ever. Why? Nowadays, unlike our ancestors, we spend less time staring into space, watching clouds go by, appreciating nature, and just being present in the moment. Put simply, the pace of life has accelerated, and generally speaking, we are all chasing our tails trying to keep up with it.

It's probably the *best* investment I *EVER* made.

Stella McCartney on meditation

THE NEED TO SLOW DOWN

There is no denying that today's seemingly non-stop world is a demanding one. We are bombarded on a daily basis with more information and stimulation than our ancestors encountered in their whole lifetimes. From high-pressure jobs, deadlines, and digital overload, to traffic chaos, an endless "to do" list, financial worries, and relationship problems, we are probably more stressed and under more pressure than at any time in the past. As a result, our stress response, one of our innate physiological mechanisms that should only be triggered in life-threatening situations, is triggered constantly. Most of us never slow down enough simply to "be."

THE PRESENT MOMENT

We are surrounded with so many things demanding our attention. Take a few minutes to focus on the essential: your feelings and thoughts. In a world where we have forgotten the value of living in the present moment, of being aware of the "here and now" and the power it holds, meditation is what we need to bring us back to ourselves.

At the end of
the day, I can end
up just totally wacky,
because I've made
mountains out of molehills.
With meditation, I can
keep them as molehills.

Ringo Starr

[MEDITATION]
HELPS ME SET
MY MOTIVATION
FOR THE DAY.

Richard Gere

HEALTH BENEFITS

The simple practice of meditation has multiple health benefits that can help alleviate the stress of modern living and bring some balance back to your world. Meditation improves brain and gut function, benefits your immunity and mood, and even helps to slow down the aging process. Taking the time every day to be still in your mind is one of the best steps you can take toward happiness and health.

It makes me calm
and happy and . . .
gives me some peace
and quiet in what's
a pretty chaotic life!

Hugh Jackman
on meditation

A SOLUTION FOR STRESS

Stress has all sorts of short- and long-term health implications. Stress-related problems can range from anxiety, digestive issues, and high blood pressure to headaches, poor sleep, and fatigue. Before going to the pharmacy and buying a packet of pills, think about giving meditation a try instead. Meditation gives mind and body the chance to recharge and renew. If you practice on a regular basis you will discover that it is one of the most effective stress-busting techniques around. Truly. No pills required.

MEDITATION IS
A LIFELONG GIFT.
IT'S SOMETHING
YOU CAN CALL ON
AT ANY TIME.

Paul McCartney

MEDICINE FOR THE MIND

When we are free of stress, we sleep well and feel happier. We feel better in every way. With practice, meditation helps dispel troubled thoughts and enables you to cultivate a deeper sense of self-awareness. People who meditate generally lead happier lives than those who do not. And quite apart from enhancing your happiness and improving your overall well-being, meditation also helps sharpen your memory and concentration levels. Can't be bad!

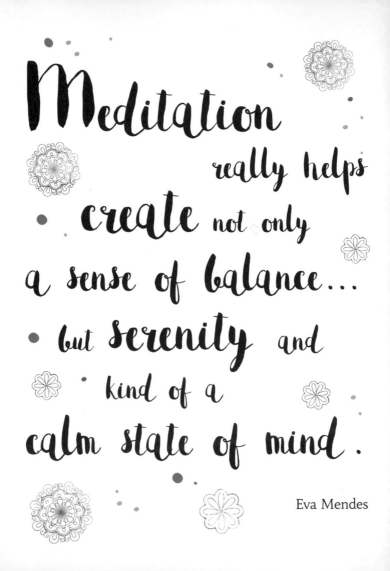

Meditation really helps create not only a sense of balance... but serenity and kind of a calm state of mind.

Eva Mendes

BRAIN TRAINING

The importance of meditation simply can't be underestimated. By focusing on moment-by-moment experiences, your brain is trained to remain calm, even in stressful situations. The anxiety caused by uncertainty of future events also reduces significantly. We all need quiet time to recharge our batteries, and nowadays meditation is enjoying the recognition it deserves for helping us to do so.

Meditation . . . helps [me] make better decisions and be a better mother, and just deal with the daily stress of the modern world.

Liv Tyler

Meditation has a calming effect that leaves us relaxed by deactivating the stress response; it allows us to achieve a deep state of rest. In this state, self-healing takes place. Can you think of a better way to cure life's ills?

a BRIEF HISTORY of MEDITATION

THE FIRST MEDITATORS

No one knows exactly when people began to meditate, but experts agree that the practice began thousands of years ago, before the birth of modern civilization.

In prehistoric times, civilizations used repetitive, rhythmic chants during offerings to their gods. Some early references to meditation are found in Hindu scriptures, while around the fifth to sixth centuries CE other forms of meditation were developed in Confucian and Taoist China and Buddhist India. The structured practice of meditation that we are more likely to recognize these days probably dates back around five thousand years ago to India. The practice as a formal element of a spiritual path is probably most closely associated with Buddhism, a spiritual tradition which has adapted to the cultures of the regions where it has taken root.

The word "meditation" comes from the Latin *meditari* (to think, to dwell upon, to contemplate, to exercise the mind) and *mederi* (to heal). The Sanskrit derivation *medha* means "wisdom."

A CALM MIND IS
NOT DISTURBED
BY THE WAVES
OF THOUGHTS.

Remez Sasson

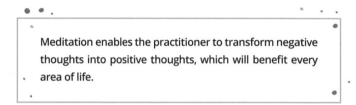

Meditation enables the practitioner to transform negative thoughts into positive thoughts, which will benefit every area of life.

A split between Hindu and Buddhist meditation came about when Buddhist followers no longer believed that meditation should be used to reach a closer understanding of a higher being, which was what Hindu meditation was for. Buddhists looked on it, rather, as a means of realizing one's interrelatedness with all things.

A calm and peaceful mind is a reservoir of creative ideas and enables you to make those ideas reality.

As Japanese Buddhism started to grow during the eighth century CE, the Japanese monk Dosho was taught Zen during a visit to China. When he came back home he opened his first meditation hall in Japan. He wrote the instructions for seated meditation, known as "Zazen," and created a community of monks who primarily focused on that form of meditation.

Meanwhile, different religious groups developed their own versions of meditation. The Jewish community incorporated certain meditative practices into their traditions, including their Kabbalistic methods. In Islam, individuals practiced breathing control while chanting the different names for Allah. Eastern Christians repeated prayers and incorporated certain meditative poses.

Meditation helps people to procrastinate less and therefore enables them to get more done in the same amount of time.

A BRIEF TIMELINE OF MEDITATION

5000–3500 BCE—According to archaeologists, who have discovered evidence of meditation in wall art in the Indus Valley in the northwest regions of southern Asia, meditation starts around this time. Images depict people sitting on the ground with crossed legs, their hands resting on their knees. Many of us recognize these as meditation postures.

1500 BCE—Earliest documented records of meditation stem from the Vedas of India.

600–500 BCE—Chinese Taoists and Indian Buddhists develop their own versions of meditation.

400–200 BCE—The *Bhagavad Gita* is written, discussing Hindu philosophy, yoga, meditation, and spiritual life.

653 CE—Dosho, a Japanese monk, opens the first meditation hall in Japan.

Fast-forward to the twentieth century, when Eastern teachings gain popularity in Western culture.

1950s—Secular forms of meditation are introduced in India as a modern form of Hindu meditative techniques.

1960s—Transcendental meditation (see page 113) becomes popular in North America and Europe. This is a time when young adults start to experiment with mind-expanding drugs. The Beatles famously popularize the change in the culture of the times when they travel to India and take up meditation, which affects them deeply enough for them to write their *White Album.*

Your vision will become clear only when you can look into your own heart.
Who looks outside, dreams; who looks inside, awakes.

Carl Jung

TYPES of MEDITATION

CHOOSING A STYLE

There are lots of different types of meditation out there for you to choose from. Some styles focus on a mantra or on your breathing, while others incorporate walking, visualizing, t'ai chi, yoga, or crystals. Everyone does it differently.

In order to find out what kind of meditation works best for you, you'll have to put a few types to the test, so you can choose the practice that you feel most comfortable with. You can't become familiar with all of them, but you will find one or two that suit you and your needs. While some people practice primarily one form of meditation, it is perfectly OK to switch between a couple of types from time to time.

Classes, books, and videos are available to help you discover what meditation can do for you. Don't be afraid to experiment with new techniques to see what best suits you and your lifestyle.

HEART RHYTHM MEDITATION (HRM)

Beneficial for: stress relief and balancing hormone levels

Heart rhythm meditation focuses energy on developing the application of consciousness. This form of meditation concentrates primarily on the heart, with an emphasis on breathing in time to a set number of heartbeats. This results in a feeling of being centered in your body with a focused mind. This type of meditation is mainly practiced while sitting with the eyes closed, although it can be done with eyes open while walking, talking, or even working. HRM provides physical, emotional, and spiritual benefits and helps the individual to better handle stress and develop an appreciative spirit.

MEDITATION ALLOWS US TO DIRECTLY PARTICIPATE IN OUR LIVES INSTEAD OF LIVING LIFE AS AN AFTERTHOUGHT.

Stephen Levine

CHAKRA MEDITATION

Beneficial for: increasing confidence, balancing emotions, and enhancing the vibration of thoughts

Chakras are the body's energy centers. There are seven of them:

1. The root chakra at the base of the spine relates to our basic needs, survival, and security.
2. The sacral chakra in the lower abdomen below the navel is all about our well-being and ability to connect to others.
3. The solar plexus chakra in the upper abdomen governs self-confidence and intellect.
4. The heart chakra, above the heart, relates to our emotions and how we show love.
5. The throat chakra, located in the neck, is all about how we communicate.
6. The third-eye chakra, between the eyebrows, represents intuition and the ability to see what lies below the surface.
7. The crown chakra, at the top of the head, is the gateway to spiritual connection.

The most common chakra meditation for those starting out involves focusing on the heart (fourth) chakra.

Close your eyes and rub the palms of your hands together to create a feeling of warmth and energy. Place your right hand on the center of your chest, over your heart chakra, and put your left hand on top of your right hand. Breathe deeply and while exhaling say "yam"—this is the vibration associated with the heart chakra. Visualize green energy radiating from your chest into your palms. When you are ready, put your hands by your sides, allowing love, life, and positivity to escape from your palms, sending your love to the world.

The other most popular chakra meditation is the third-eye chakra, known as *anja chakra* in Sanskrit. This chakra is located between your eyebrows and is connected to intuition, imagination, and the ability to see our connection to the bigger picture.

A FREE AND
SILENT MIND
IS ALWAYS IN
MEDITATION.

Remez Sasson

KUNDALINI

**Beneficial for: increasing physical energy and
dealing with issues such as fibromyalgia**

Kundalini, translated into English, means "serpent"
or "snake." This rather complex form of meditation,
which is also a type of yoga, has its roots in Buddhist
and Hindu teachings. It focuses on awakening, thereby
releasing the *Kundalini* energy that lies dormant in the
triangular sacrum at the lower end of the spine. It does
this by concentrating on breathing as it flows through
energy centers in the body. Evoking this energy purifies
the system and brings about complete awareness of
your body. In *Kundalini*, techniques such as breathing
through alternate nostrils may be used. Once that
energy is released, the individual can experience an
altered state of consciousness. *Kundalini* involves intense
breath work and opening the root chakra, and its end
goals include cleansing the mind, increasing physical
vitality, balancing chakras, increasing consciousness,
and ultimately achieving enlightenment.

It is recommended that you only practice *Kundalini*
meditation in the presence of an experienced yogi.

Meditation helps
us realize that the
most important
gift we have is the
here and now.

GUIDED VISUALIZATION

Beneficial for: self-improvement, healing, stress relief, and personal development

This technique can be used for spiritual healing, stress relief, or personal development: "The mind is everything. What you think you become," so says a Buddhist proverb. By imagining happy, positive experiences, the body responds by releasing chemicals that generate feelings of positivity. These visualizations are usually tailored to help you accomplish specific goals, from sporting achievements to personal transformation or deep relaxation. Guided visualization can help you experience a deeper spiritual connection or access your subconscious mind; almost any aspect of one's life can be improved by the use of positive imagery. If you have a specific goal in mind, practicing guided visualization is very straightforward: you simply visualize yourself in your desired situation.

Visualization meditations belonging to the Tibetan tradition are generally specific religious practices. During these practices, visualizing a meditation deity gives practitioners a basis for cultivating inner qualities such as compassion and wisdom. For this kind of practice, instructions should be given by a professional yogi.

BE THE MASTER
OF MIND RATHER
THAN MASTERED
BY MIND.

Japanese proverb

Print out your favorite meditation quotes. Pin them on a wall by your desk, on the fridge, in the bathroom, or somewhere prominent so that you see them several times every day. The more often you read them, the more effective they will become; eventually they will seem like second nature to you.

ZAZEN

**Beneficial for: stress-busting, improving creativity
and awareness, enhancing mental and physical health**

"Zazen" or "Zen" meditation is the heart of Zen Buddhist practice and translates as "seated meditation." The psychological benefits are huge, because the aim is to forget judgmental thoughts and ideas. Zazen develops insight into how your body and mind operate.

Sit on the floor with legs in the lotus position. How your head is positioned is important—you should hold it in a natural position that does not put any strain on your neck. Be aware of any tension in your facial muscles, and focus on breathing through your nose. Pay attention to the natural rhythm and the warm and cold sensations of the air passing through your nose and lungs.

Meditation is a blanket term for an ever-growing group of disciplines. Most meditation methods involve finding a quiet space, holding your body in a specific posture, and focusing your thoughts, thereby achieving a state of positivity, openness, and enlightenment.

MINDFULNESS

Beneficial for: improving self-control, concentration, and sharpening memory

What is mindfulness? Put simply, it is about paying attention to life in a purposeful way—a way of living in the here and now, without judgment. It is about acknowledging reality by letting the mind wander, accepting any thoughts that come along, and staying rooted in the present. It helps practitioners to be themselves and learn to live in the moment through posture and breathing work. It is the practice of intentionally focusing on the present moment, on internal and external experiences, accepting and non-judgmentally paying attention to the sensations, thoughts, and emotions that arise. In this way, practitioners gain a calmness and appreciation for life as it happens. The overall essence of mindfulness is being gentle, appreciative, and nurturing.

Mindfulness meditation makes life more enjoyable, vivid, and fulfilling. The intention is not to get involved with the thoughts that fly through your brain nor to criticize them, but simply to be aware of each mental note as it arises. Through this type of meditation, you can see how your thoughts and feelings tend to move in patterns. With practice, an inner balance develops. Mindfulness allows you to be present in the moment by bringing your attention to various sensations within your body. Start by focusing on your breath then let yourself become aware of other sensations— for example, how you are sitting, where you feel tension, or how relaxed you feel. Try not to analyze any thought that passes through your mind or judge anything you experience: simply observe.

If you are constantly worried about the future or find you become upset or hurt by doubts and past events, you might appreciate mindfulness techniques. Mindfulness meditation isn't about letting your thoughts wander, neither is it about trying to empty your mind. Instead, the practice involves paying close attention to the present moment—especially thoughts, emotions, and sensations. When this happens, simply notice what it is you were thinking about or what was distracting you, then take a moment and pause. You don't need to pull your attention right back to the breath. Instead, let go of whatever it was you were thinking about, reopen your attention, then gently return your awareness to the breath, being present for each inhalation and exhalation. Learn to enjoy your practice. When you are finished, appreciate how different your body and mind feel.

You can also apply mindfulness meditation to your daily activities—for example, while you're watching TV, enjoying a workout at the gym, or sitting at your desk. In fact, anything you do can provide the opportunity to practice mindfulness: be mindful of your breathing; ground your awareness in the present moment. Your senses will become sharper, and your mind will grow more attuned to subtle details.

To practice mindfulness in your day-to-day life, pay attention to what is going on in the here and now instead of functioning in "automatic mode." While speaking, pay attention to the words you say. When listening to someone else speak, do so attentively. While walking, be aware of how your body moves and what sounds happen to be going on around you. While eating, note the texture and taste of every bite you take.

I KNOW BUT
ONE FREEDOM
AND THAT IS THE
FREEDOM OF
THE MIND.

Antoine de
Saint-Exupéry

LOVING KINDNESS MEDITATION (LKM)

**Beneficial for: increasing happiness and helping
to reduce feelings of anger or resentment**

Also called "metta" or "compassion" meditation, LKM aims to cultivate an attitude of unconditional love and kindness toward others. To achieve this you must first generate feelings of unconditional love for yourself. While breathing deeply, practitioners open their minds to receiving loving kindness and send messages of loving kindness to the world. Buddhists say, "May I be happy. May I be peaceful." You could say, "May I be filled with the grace and love of the universe." Feel free to repeat words and phrases that feel right for you.

First of all, direct your loving kindness feelings to someone you like, then practice directing those feelings to someone you feel neither friendly nor unfriendly toward. Finally, and this is the hardest part, direct the feelings to someone you have negative feelings for. It will take time—of course it will—but eventually you will begin to be able to open your heart to allow loving kindness in, even in challenging circumstances. As you practice more and more, you will finally be able to hold loving feelings for those people who stir anger or other negative thoughts.

When you feel angry, perhaps about something someone has said or done, don't refuse to acknowledge this emotion—observe it for what it is. Consider how it makes you feel. Do you feel a tight knot in your stomach? Are your thoughts overtaken by this feeling of anger? Accept the thoughts for what they are. Anger is simply an emotion, like all others.

CONCENTRATION MEDITATION

Beneficial for: improving concentration and living in the moment

Also known as "focused attention meditation," this involves focusing on a single point or object. It could entail repeating a mantra, focusing on a candle flame, or counting numbers using a *mala* (a Sanskrit word for prayer beads). A beginner might meditate for a few minutes to start with, before gradually increasing the time. In this form of meditation, you refocus your awareness each time you notice your mind wandering. This technique calls for an absolute focus on a physical sensation, such as air entering and leaving the lungs or the temperature of your hands. For many, this allows the mind to let go of scattered thoughts and provides relief from sensory overload.

Do you feel your body growing tense when you meditate? If so, it is probably because you are distracted by existing thoughts. The way to resolve this is by meditating more often.

PRIMORDIAL SOUND MEDITATION (PSM)

**Beneficial for: strengthening the immune system,
providing an increased sense of well-being,
and providing greater energy and creativity**

A key component of PSM is the mantra—a word or sound which is repeated to aid concentration. The mantra is the specific sound or vibration that helps you move into a state of simultaneous calm and awareness. When you learn PSM, your teacher will give you a personal mantra which is the vibration the universe was creating at the time and place of your birth.

Practice your mantra on a daily basis to help guide you from the turmoil of daily activities toward stillness. Primordial sounds are the basic vibrations of nature— for instance, wind, sea, our breathing. Others are silent vibrations, such as the sounds of plants growing, the Earth rotating, or the silent rhythms of our bodies that we sense internally. PSM encourages you to use silence to experience inner calm, which is perfect for dealing with the stresses of our world today and promoting peaceful sleep. Silence is the birthplace of happiness, creativity, and infinite possibility.

VIPASSANA MEDITATION

Beneficial for: absolute inner transformation

Vipassana is the oldest Buddhist meditation practice, dating back to the sixth century BCE. It can be translated as "insight," a clear awareness of exactly what is happening as it happens.

It is a gentle but thorough practice, rooted in discipline. Unlike mindfulness meditation, which focuses on awareness, *Vipassana* is an excellent meditation technique to help you ground yourself within your body and in time, enabling you to understand how the processes of your mind work. It has five basic principles that practitioners must follow:

1. Abstain from killing any living organism.
2. Do not steal.
3. Shun sexual misconduct.
4. Make sure you are not using the power of language in wrong ways.
5. Refrain from any intoxicants.

This is a meditation method best taught by a teacher in a class or retreat to ensure proper guidance is given.

MANTRAS

The mantra is an instrument that creates vibrations in the mind, enabling disconnection from your thoughts and allowing you to enter a deeper state of consciousness.

Some of those who practice meditation like to repeat a mantra. This is not an affirmation used to convince yourself of something. Mantras are effective as long as you channel positive feelings while using them. Feel, desire, accept that what you want will happen. Supercharge your desire. Manifest your wishes by using your thoughts, and speed up the receiving process. If you merely repeat your mantra unconsciously without depth of feeling, then don't be surprised if nothing much changes.

The word "mantra" comes from Sanskrit and means "tool or instrument of thought." This syllable or word, usually without any particular meaning, is repeated for the purpose of focusing your mind.

Mantras employ the thinking mind instead of trying to ignore it or silence it. You are employing the mind by giving it something to do—repeating aloud or silently a particular word or phrase to focus, relax, and dispel mental distractions. Traditionally, mantras were bestowed by a seasoned teacher. Maharishi Mahesh Yogi taught that each individual instructed in meditation should have their mantra chosen by a trained teacher, in order for it to be suitable for that person and to produce the best results.

Om (or *aum*) is a popular mantra; chanting it can create a feeling of wholeness and an expanded experience of reality. It is made up of three sounds and each one—A, U, and M—is said to have its own significance and meaning.

Some of the most well-known mantras from the Hindu tradition are *om so-ham*, which means "I am that," *om namah shivaya*, which shows adoration to Lord Shiva, and *ram*, which is repeated as a way to show devotion and commitment to acting justly, with wisdom and compassion for all. Or you could use the phrase *Sat, Chit, Ananda*, which means "Existence, Consciousness, Bliss." It's important to use a mantra that feels right for you, perhaps one that you feel will help you grow stronger or that helps you feel calm and enables you to focus on the present.

MANTRA MEDITATION

Beneficial for: lowering blood pressure and heart rate, decreasing anxiety and depression, and providing greater feelings of relaxation and general well-being

Mantra meditation is where you continually repeat a chosen word or phrase. It is ideal for those people whose mind is always chattering. There are some who find it easier to focus with a mantra than with breathing. Because a mantra is a word, and thoughts are usually perceived as words, it can be easier to keep the focus on a mantra. It is useful especially when the mind is racing with many thoughts. Transcendental meditation (see page 113) is also a type of mantra meditation, as are mindfulness, yoga, t'ai chi, and qigong.

When you practice mantra meditation, your mind doesn't have time to flutter from one thought to the next, as its focus is solely on repeating the mantra.

By repeating a mantra, either silently or aloud, you can bring your mind to a state of focused tranquillity by slowing the nervous system and transporting the mind beyond its usual thought patterns. As with other types of meditation, mantra meditation requires practice.

If you find it hard at first, persevere and don't give up—it can bring positive changes to your life. If you know exactly why you want to practice mantra meditation, it will help you identify the best affirmations for you to chant. One of the goals of chanting mantras is to feel their subtle vibrations. This sensation can help you effect positive changes and enter a deep state of meditation. Each mantra has different vibrations, and you need to find one that corresponds to your intention. Repeating mantras can help you disconnect from thoughts that arise during meditation and also help keep you focused on your intention.

To experiment with how mantra meditation might suit you, choose a phrase or a single word with deep personal meaning and repeat it over and over again, focusing on the sound and the feeling it evokes. Traditionally, a teacher would give you a mantra for your use only and you would not tell anyone what that word or phrase is.

The ancient Sanskrit word *om* (or *aum*) is a mystical syllable often used in chants or as a meditative mantra. As a meditative mantra it has great symbolism and power. When om is chanted in a class, the sense of togetherness created through the shared sound is powerful.

TRANSCENDENTAL MEDITATION (TM)

Beneficial for: reducing blood pressure and depression, and helping to strengthen coping skills

Transcendental meditation was popularized in the 1950s and 1960s by Maharishi Mahesh Yogi, and it explores the power of sounds and vibrations to engage and enlighten. Maharishi defined its goal as "the state of enlightenment. This means we experience that inner calmness, that quiet state of least excitation, even when we are dynamically busy." TM involves the use of a mantra and is practiced for fifteen or twenty minutes, twice a day, with your eyes closed. In this Hindu tradition, you sit in the lotus position, silently chant a mantra, and focus on rising above negative thoughts. The mantra is not unique, in contrast to mantra meditation; in TM the mantra is based on the practitioner's gender and age. These are also not "meaningless sounds" but are Tantric names of Hindu deities. For beginners, the repetition of words and sounds helps focus the mind.

TM is another form of meditation where expert guidance is recommended. Look for classes, internet resources, or meditation retreats to better learn this form of meditation. In some retreats you can spend a couple of days, a week, or more concentrating on learning a particular type of meditation or trying out different types.

Transcendental meditation is something that can be defined as a means to do what one wants to do in a better way, a right way, for maximum results.

Maharishi Mahesh Yogi

MEDITATING WITH CRYSTALS

Beneficial for: increasing energy and improving self-image

Before setting out on a crystal meditation, make sure you have cleansed your crystals or precious stones. Find a quiet place where you will not be disturbed, then sit with the crystals or stones that you wish to use. Recommended crystals for this type of meditation are quartz crystals and selenite crystals. Quartz crystals help bring clarity of the mind and encourage you to become more focused. They also have the benefit of amplifying the energy of other crystals. Selenite is beneficial because its healing properties facilitate the release of negative energy and blockages while protecting the body's energy field. Choosing a crystal with stripes or patterns within it may help you to "lose yourself" within the crystal while meditating.

As far as stones go, palm stones or touchstones (which fit inside the palm of your hand) are good for both beginners and seasoned meditators. While you meditate, hold one crystal or stone in each hand and feel their energy flowing into your body.

Close your eyes and quiet your mind. Focus your attention on your breathing; make each out-breath a little longer than the in-breath. Open your eyes, then pick up the crystals or stones and hold them gently in your hands. Look at them. Concentrate and take note of the color, pattern, and shape, then imagine your awareness spiralling into the crystal or stone, feeling its energy. Imagine you are inside your crystal; let yourself move with its flow. Let go of thoughts and move deep into the crystal's center, admiring its inner beauty. When you feel ready, slowly let yourself return to the here and now. Put your crystals or stones aside and ground yourself by imagining roots coming from your feet and burrowing deep into the ground. You may want to lie down at this stage and place your crystals or stones on their associated chakra.

**INNER STILLNESS
IS THE KEY TO
OUTER STRENGTH.**

Jared Brock

ACTIVE MEDITATION: QIGONG

Beneficial for: reducing fibromyalgia pain and chronic neck pain, as well as levelling blood pressure

Qigong combines posture, movement, breathing technique, and sound to improve mental and physical health. As one of the oldest forms of meditation, qigong is still as popular as ever, because it helps improve posture and assists relaxation. Qigong is designed to raise self-awareness and balance life energy by exploring the connection between body, mind, and spirit. This meditation form uses breath to circulate energy through the body and energy centers.

There are two primary types of qigong practice: one is Wai Dan, which involves physical movement and concentration; the other is Nei Dan, which uses seated meditation and guided imagery and visualization. The focused combination to breathing techniques, movement, and meditation helps the individual to control their reaction to stress. This is a low-impact way to move through postures and stretches that focus on mindfulness. You will move through various positions while practicing and have space to stretch your arms. Posture is important in qigong, and your spine should be straight.

ACTIVE MEDITATION: YOGA

Beneficial for: increasing positive energy and improving mood

Although yoga and meditation are two separate practices, they support each other. To that end, some yoga instructors even reserve time at the beginning or end of a yoga class to practice some form of meditation. There is not one specific type of yogic meditation, but there are several meditation types taught in the yoga tradition. The posture and concentration required during yoga aids focus and balance, helping to promote a more flexible body. Moving through the poses encourages the practitioner to focus less on general issues and more on the moment. The physical component of yoga and its emphasis on *ujjayi* breathing* helps to set aside concerns and worries, which is deeply meditative.

*When practicing *ujjayi*, completely fill your lungs with air while contracting your throat slightly and breathing through your nose.

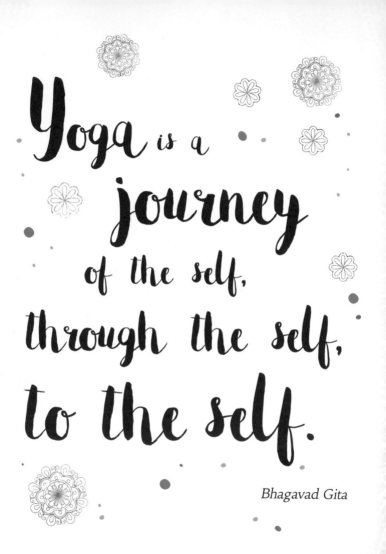

Yoga is a *journey* of the self, through the self, to the self.

Bhagavad Gita

One yogic meditation is the breathing exercise called *Pranayama*, which comes from the words *Prana* meaning "life force or breath sustaining the body" and *Ayama*, which translates as "to extend or draw out." To be absolutely precise, it is not exactly meditation, but it is a great practice for calming the mind and preparing it for meditation. The easiest type of *Pranayama* is the 4–4–4–4 which involves breathing in through your nose and counting up to four, holding that for four counts, breathing out for four counts, and holding empty for four counts. This helps balance the mood and calms both mind and body. A big advantage is that it can be done anywhere.

ACTIVE MEDITATION: T'AI CHI

Beneficial for: improving strength and balance

Like yoga, t'ai chi alone is not meditation. Sometimes referred to as "meditation in motion," t'ai chi utilizes ancient practices that focus on the physical and spiritual aspects of life. This form of gentle Chinese martial arts combines deep breathing and relaxation with slow and gentle movements. Among them are two methods, neigong and qigong, which concentrate on life energy. Both emphasize the importance of body posture, breathing, and meditation to restore energy, or "chi." Originally developed in thirteenth-century China as a martial art, today t'ai chi is practiced worldwide. The deliberate, orchestrated, controlled movements and intense concentration required help still the mind and bring a deeper sense of relaxation, which releases inner tension and increases awareness.

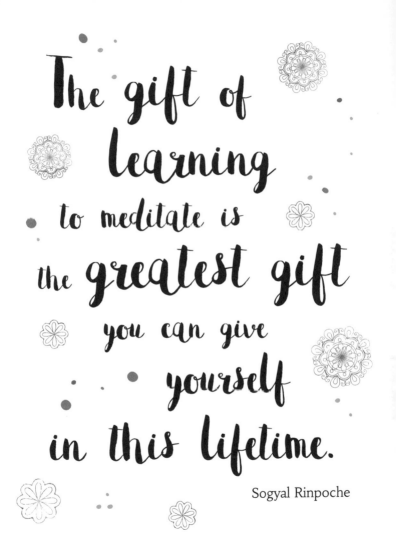

The gift of
learning
to meditate is
the greatest gift
you can give
yourself
in this lifetime.

Sogyal Rinpoche

WALKING MEDITATION

Beneficial for: relieving anxiety and promoting personal growth

For those who find it hard to stay still for any length of time, or who just enjoy being on the move, this is an ideal form of meditation. While walking is not the only form of moving meditation, it is one of the most popular. This is something you can do anywhere, although doing so in a pleasant environment such as a park, garden, or on a quiet beach is ideal. If that is not possible, choose somewhere that is not too busy or noisy and has as few distractions as possible. Depending on where you walk, you may prefer to remove your shoes.

Start off by taking a slow, deliberate step with your right foot. Forget about any sensations or feelings in the foot, and try to concentrate on the movement itself. After taking the first step, stop for a moment before taking the next. Only one foot should be moving at any given time. Focus on your arms as they swing, your legs as they lift, your feet as they rise and touch the ground. As with all meditation techniques, when you find your mind wandering, gently bring your attention back to the movement, to each step you take. Just observe the sensation of walking.

While practicing walking meditation, try to focus on the movement of the feet. This intense focus is similar to the way that you concentrate on the rising and falling of your breath during breathing meditation. Try to clear your mind and become aware of the connection between your foot and the ground beneath it. This uses aspects of the concentration meditation technique, and supporters say it is easier for some people to focus on the sensation of air on your skin while you walk. Do not worry about how far you walk or where you end up—the focus on steps and breathing is what is important here, as is becoming aware of your body's connection to the Earth.

When meditation
is mastered, the mind
is unwavering like the
flame of a candle in a
windless place.

Bhagavad Gita

EMPTY MIND MEDITATION

Beneficial for: imbuing body and mind with a sense of calm

This meditation technique allows you to be aware without any specific focus, but it has to be said that it is very difficult to achieve. Sit quietly either in the full or half lotus position, or on a straight-backed chair with your eyes closed. Observe your breathing, counting your breaths from one to nine, and then begin counting again at one. Allow thoughts to float freely in and out of your mind. As they come and go, observe them without judgment until you experience a gap, however small, between two thoughts where there is no thought. Focus gently on those gaps, making them last longer until there are no further thoughts. Buddha used this method to reach enlightenment.

Of course, this takes effort and perseverance over many, many years of practice—but if you are determined to succeed with this method, you will eventually get there.

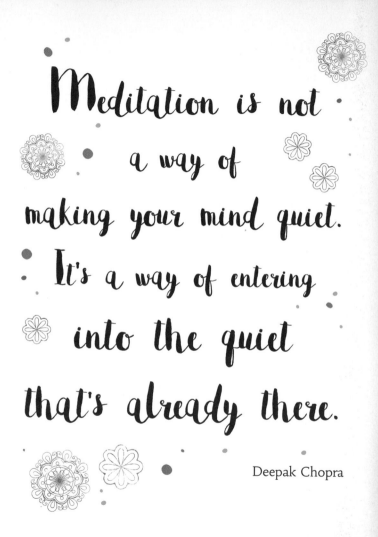

Meditation is not
a way of
making your mind quiet.
It's a way of entering
into the quiet
that's already there.

Deepak Chopra

The BENEFITS of MEDITATION

A CALMER MIND AND A HEALTHIER BODY

Meditation benefits your mental and physical health; there is no doubt at all that it helps reduce stress and anxiety while also helping to banish the blues. When you focus on moment-by-moment experiences, over time your brain is being trained to remain calm even in the most stressful situations. Anxiety caused by day-to-day doubts or uncertainty about future events also reduces significantly.

Meditation plays an important part in our well-being by enabling us to eliminate negative thoughts and worries.

GREATER FOCUS

Here is something else that might encourage you to meditate if you are not quite sure yet that it is for you: people who meditate are generally happier than those who don't. This is because meditation enhances the flow of constructive thoughts and positive emotions.

Apart from enhancing your happiness and improving your overall well-being, meditation also helps sharpen your memory and improves your concentration levels. Consequently, you will find you get less distracted. Those silly mistakes we often make—such as misplacing keys or forgetting the time of an appointment—become less frequent once you start meditating.

Studies also show that multiple meditation styles can increase memory, mental quickness, and attention in older volunteers. Besides helping to combat normal memory loss, some think meditation may partially improve memory in Alzheimer's patients. It can also help control stress and improve coping ability for those who are caretakers for family members with dementia.

IMPROVED HEALTH

Even though meditation should not be considered a cure by itself, research has shown it to be beneficial for a wide range of health problems, both mental and physical. Because it is a stress-managing technique, meditation can boost the immune system and lower blood cholesterol. The latter, a result of diet and genetics, is often affected by chronic stress. Meditation helps to make us feel calmer and can regulate blood pressure to the extent that, in some cases, it can be an alternative to blood-pressure medication for those with moderate hypertension. (Don't ditch your meds straightaway though—always check with your doctor or pharmacist before stopping any prescribed medications.)

Meditation promotes a positive state of mind, including happiness and well-being, and encourages the flow of life energy. This enhances self-confidence and effectiveness.

We are all looking to find inner peace in our often hectic lives. After all, isn't inner peace the key to feeling good, positive, and happy? Of course, we all know that exercising regularly, eating sensibly, and practicing positive thinking all help, but meditation is one of the prime ways to achieve this feel-good state of mind. The psychological benefits of meditation are far-reaching, and as is the case with most things, the more you practice, the more benefits you experience.

WHERE THERE
IS PEACE AND
MEDITATION, THERE
IS NEITHER ANXIETY
NOR DOUBT.

Saint Francis
of Assisi

STAY YOUNG THROUGH MEDITATION

Studies into the effects of meditation show that practicing regularly can slow the aging process. Generally speaking, the biological age of long-term meditators is lower than that of those who have never meditated. Those in the know say this is because meditation helps reduce the body's production of free radicals, which are organic molecules responsible for aging.

The effect of meditation on physical and mental health cannot be underestimated. There are many psychological benefits, including improved learning ability, memory, and concentration. Besides that, meditation increases productivity and provides emotional stability.

THE JOURNEY

As soon as you set out on your meditation journey, you will begin to see some benefits. You will probably achieve a sense of calmness and peace of mind quite early on in your journey. You might feel more relaxed, less stressed, and find that things don't faze you quite so much. Even if this feeling is subtle, make no mistake it is there. Issues such as anxiety and depression gradually become more manageable as you progress further with your meditation journey.

Even if relaxation is not your end goal of meditation, it is often a result.

MEDITATIONS for a VARIETY of COMMON ISSUES

WHY WE MEDITATE

We all have different reasons for meditating. For some, it could be to help soothe away stress or anxiety, quell inner turmoil, improve relationships, or determine a path in life. It could be to awaken to the present or to make friends with yourself. For others, it may even be to dispel feelings of anger or be able to act calmly in difficult situations. Some people do it to help improve their creativity, others to help them to visualize a certain goal they may aspire to.

One thing is certain: meditation is important to our well-being. Of course, maybe you meditate so that you can enjoy a few minutes of relaxation.

With meditation you will also learn how to promote certain other qualities and skills to bring improvements to your favorite pastime or venture—whether that is playing tennis, gardening, or achieving something business-related.

MEDITATION TO
FIND SIMPLICITY IN LIFE

Just think about it—the less you have in life, the less you have to worry about. However, achieving a simpler life is easier said than done. Meditation helps internalize the benefits of simplicity in life; an immediate result of making the decision to focus on simplicity is relief from anxiety, because instantly there are fewer problems to address.

As you meditate: Visualize life without the extras. What can you do without? Would you really miss those things, or would there be more space in your life for joy as your material possessions decrease? Increase your meditation focus on intangibles—for example, love, caring, beauty, peace—instead of giving mental power to possessions. Give yourself permission to trade the joy of having for the joy of not having.

What we are
today comes from our
thoughts of yesterday,
and present thoughts build
our life of tomorrow: our
life is the creation of our
own mind.

Buddhist proverb

MEDITATION FOR
CALMING MENTAL CHAOS

Mental chaos—that constant chatter in the brain—may cause physical stress, a common side-effect of anxiety. It seems that the harder we try to quiet the mental chatter, the less effective it is. The more muddled everything becomes, the more we feel anxious. Meditation can help your brain break the habit of excessive multitasking. It reduces anxiety and strengthens your ability to regulate your emotions.

As you meditate: Breathe in to invite space into your entire body, and then breathe out to release tension. Meditation techniques can be used to adopt an attitude of acceptance. No matter what happens, you can give yourself permission to be peaceful. Use meditation to visualize yourself floating with serenity above any conflict.

Meditation calms and soothes your soul. It is one of the best habits around for encouraging a peaceful mind.

MEDITATION FOR RELAXING MIND AND BODY

Anxiety and stress cause the body to tense up, and of course we all know that our bodies do not work as well when we feel anxious or worried. Practicing meditation breaks this vicious cycle by creating a state of mind in which the body naturally lets go of the tension preventing you from relaxing. Meditation can also be used to promote healing after surgery or traumatic events.

As you meditate: Try clenching your muscles tightly as you breathe in, then releasing the tension as you breathe out.

THE THING
ABOUT MEDITATION
IS THAT YOU BECOME
MORE AND MORE
YOU.

David Lynch

MEDITATION TO
IMPROVE SELF-ESTEEM

It is easy to be self-critical in a culture obsessed with perfection. Feeling dissatisfied with your looks, body shape, and mental ability, and perhaps constantly feeling there is too much to do and not enough time to do it, can all combine to drain your self-esteem. But the more understanding and patient you are with yourself, the more attractive you will be to others. It is essential to acknowledge your strengths.

Meditation can help transform a lack of self-esteem into inner confidence, self-acceptance, and self-belief, because it allows us to meet and make friends with ourselves. It teaches us who we are and how to love ourselves exactly as we are.

As you meditate: Take a few deep breaths and pay attention to the flow of your breath as it enters and leaves your body. Focus on your heart—as you breathe in, feel your heart opening like a flower petal; when you breathe out, release all tension. Bring into your heart either an image of yourself or repeat your name. Silently tell yourself, "I love myself totally at this moment." Keep breathing into your heart and repeating the words. This will generate kindness and appreciation for yourself, which will increase the more you practice this meditation.

> Meditation is a practical tool for helping us cope with life and for nurturing personal growth. It puts things into perspective and enables us to make better decisions.

MEDITATION TO REDUCE ANXIETY

We all experience general feelings of anxiety from time to time—it's something that really cannot be avoided. Problems arise when we become overwhelmed by anxiety and when it stops us from moving forward with our lives. Prolonged anxiety is damaging to physical and mental health and can cause insomnia, irritability, and fatigue. With meditation you can learn to dispel these feelings, manage symptoms, and cope with panic attacks.

As you meditate: Mentally say "relax" each time you breathe in and each time you breathe out. When your thoughts wander, as they probably will, focus again on the word "relax." Keep repeating this word and you will start to notice how relaxed and calm you are becoming. Now just allow your mind to drift—there is no need to focus on anything at all. All you have to do is simply relax and enjoy this experience.

When daily pressures threaten to engulf you, look to the inner sanctum of your mind.

MEDITATION TO INCREASE POSITIVITY

Sometimes it is easy to fall into a negative thought pattern, but meditation can help to counter it. Positive thinking meditations help to clear your mind of clutter and banish negative thoughts that worry, annoy, or upset you. People who can think positively can also cope better with stress, are less likely to suffer from depression, and can better deal with problems at work.

As you meditate: There is a simple technique called the "stop" technique. Think of all the "shoulds" and "needs" that invade your thoughts: "I should be better at what I do;" "I need to improve in all areas;" "I should be able to complete this without a struggle." This kind of negative thinking can lead to lost sleep, bad moods, and unhappy relationships. Mentally tell these thoughts to "stop." Positive thinking will also counter negative emotions and improve your mood, leading to more positive life patterns. And of course, with each new positive thought, you remove space for the possibility of one more negative thought.

Meditation helps increase confidence and improve focus, concentration, and productivity. It can enhance your mood, increase compassion, and promote greater creativity. It also enhances your ability to live in the moment, deal with difficult situations more easily, and limit negative thoughts.

MEDITATION TO
IMPROVE GENERAL HEALTH

Whether we are dealing with symptoms of chronic illness or simply feel we would like a health boost to restore vitality and pump up our energy levels, meditation can help us learn how to mobilize our inner resources. It can reduce anxiety and allow the mind to rest in silence and space, allowing time for recovery.

As you meditate: Visualize yourself in good health—see a radiance surrounding your entire body. Now imagine all of your muscles relaxing and feel a healthy, healing energy flowing through your body from your head to your toes.

Meditation
brings wisdom;
lack of meditation
leaves ignorance. Know
well what leads you forward
and what holds you back,
and choose the path that
leads to wisdom.

Buddha

MEDITATION FOR CULTIVATING MINDFULNESS

Mindfulness means becoming aware of everything around you—sights, sounds, smells, places you find yourself in, and the people who surround you. Make no judgments. Simply allow yourself to see, hear, touch, smell, and feel. Mindfulness meditation provides perspective and breaks the cycle of worry and anxiety that occurs when your focus is on narrow thoughts with no connection to the rest of the world. It helps people change the way they think and feel about experiences—stressful ones, in particular. By paying attention to your thoughts and feelings, you become more aware of them and therefore find that you are better able to manage them.

As you meditate: Visualize yourself. Watch yourself meditate and notice everything around you in the room. Mindfulness expands your awareness of other people and enhances relationships, which in turn helps to relieve stress and anxiety.

WORDS ARE
BUT THE SHELL;
MEDITATION IS
THE KERNEL.

Bahya ibn Paquda

MEDITATION TO RELEASE JUDGMENT

Sometimes it is hard not to judge. We know it is not right to judge others, so we often judge ourselves instead—this can lead to us feeling anxious, worried, strained, and unhappy. Meditation helps us release the judgment and anxiety we feel and lets us allow others to be who they are. Not having to judge anyone or anything is a relief and frees our minds to focus on more peaceful things.

As you meditate: Briefly acknowledge all judgmental thoughts that enter your mind, then simply release them and refocus on your meditation. As you meditate, practice witnessing without judgment. The more you practice, the easier it gets to replace judgment with compassion. Consider trying karma yoga, which focuses your meditation on serving others rather than judging them.

Sacred smoke has been used for centuries to help induce meditation. If you want to try this, then choose a scent of incense that resonates with you—one that will help you find peace as you enter a meditative state.

MEDITATION TO
ENCOURAGE PEACEFUL SLEEP

We probably all know what it's like to go to bed hoping for a good night's sleep yet finding ourselves still lying there wide awake a few hours later. The longer we lie there, the more worried we become about not being able to fall asleep. It can be a vicious circle. Maybe you just cannot doze off, no matter how tired you feel. Or maybe you drop off into a troubled slumber only to wake up in the middle of the night, unable to get back to sleep again. When it is time to get up the next morning you feel tired, you are not ready to face the day ahead—and of course there is always the worry that the same thing will happen again that night.

The reasons for finding it difficult to drop off are many, but the most common reason is stress. This could be due to an overactive mind, pressures at work, or any one of a number of external factors. Worry not—meditation can and will help all those insomniacs out there to drift off peacefully into the Land of Nod.

As you meditate: Mentally let go of fear, worry, anger, and blame. Release anxiety and stress, and let go of negative thoughts. Know that your sleep will be peaceful and your dreams filled with love. Imagine closing your eyes, enjoying a good night's sleep, and waking in the morning completely refreshed and eager to begin a new day. You could repeat an affirmation— for example, "Love, happiness, and comfort abide in my soul. My mind is still. I am tranquil, relaxed. I welcome a good night's sleep." Choose an affirmation that suits you, something you can resonate with, and repeat it several times before you're ready to fall asleep.

SLEEP IS THE
GOLDEN CHAIN
THAT TIES HEALTH
AND OUR BODIES
TOGETHER.

Thomas Dekker

A LAST WORD

Now that you have come to the end of *The Little Book of Meditations*, you know you have a practice you can call upon in times of need. You have learned that regular meditation helps you feel centered, increases creativity and mental alertness, and provides an oasis of calm that is often hard to find in our world today. As you continue with your meditation sessions, you will see the beneficial effect they have on your mental clarity, and issues that seem confusing or daunting will potentially become much more manageable.

I wish you well on your meditation journey, and if reading this book has helped improve your life and your thoughts, why not give it to others as a gift? It may help them, too.

Finally, when you meditate it is important to remember that these sessions are only one part of living a balanced life. Meditation should not be used to withdraw from life. And it is important that if you or someone you know suffers from a mental illness of any kind, meditation should only be used under expert guidance.

FURTHER RESOURCES

Brooks, Jennifer
The Meditation Transformation: How to Relax and Revitalize Your Body, Your Work, and Your Perspective Today
(2014, Empowerment Nation)

Dienstmann, Giovanni
Practical Meditation: A Simple Step-by-Step Guide
(2018, DK)

Hagen, Steve
Meditation Now or Never
(2012, Penguin)

Williams, Will
The Effortless Mind: Meditation for the Modern World
(2018, Simon & Schuster)

IMAGE CREDITS